W9-BBN-566

MONEY BASICS

FINDING A JOB

by Emma Huddleston

BrightPoint Press

San Diego, CA

BrightP◇int Press

© 2020 BrightPoint Press
an imprint of ReferencePoint Press, Inc.
Printed in the United States

For more information, contact:
BrightPoint Press
PO Box 27779
San Diego, CA 92198
www.BrightPointPress.com

LIBRARY OF CONGRESS CATALOGING-IN-PUBLICATION DATA

Names: Huddleston, Emma, author.
Title: Finding a job / Emma Huddleston.
Description: San Diego, CA : ReferencePoint Press, 2020. | Series: Money basics | Includes
    bibliographical references and index. | Audience: Grades 10-12.
Identifiers: LCCN 2019034008 (print) | LCCN 2019034009 (eBook) | ISBN 9781682827994
    (hardcover) | ISBN 9781682828007 (eBook)
Subjects: LCSH: Job hunting--Juvenile literature. | Employment interviewing--Juvenile
    literature.
Classification: LCC HF5382.7 .H83 2020 (print) | LCC HF5382.7 (eBook) | DDC 650.14--
    dc23
LC record available at https://lccn.loc.gov/2019034008
LC ebook record available at https://lccn.loc.gov/2019034009

CONTENTS

INTRODUCTION   4
WHAT IS THE RIGHT JOB FOR ME?

CHAPTER ONE   10
WHERE CAN I FIND JOB OPENINGS?

CHAPTER TWO   24
WHAT DO I NEED TO APPLY FOR A JOB?

CHAPTER THREE   38
HOW DO I APPLY FOR A JOB?

CHAPTER FOUR   52
HOW DOES A JOB INTERVIEW WORK?

CHAPTER FIVE   64
I GOT A JOB OFFER! NOW WHAT?

Worksheet   72
Glossary   74
Source Notes   75
For Further Research   76
Index   78
Image Credits   79
About the Author   80

WHAT IS THE RIGHT JOB FOR ME?

Julia clicks the button on her car keys. Beep! The car is locked. She walks into her house. She has been driving for several months. However, her parents recently told her she needs to help pay for gas. Paying for gas is a way to take responsibility for her driving.

Many students get a job to pay for expenses such as gas.

Julia plans to get a job. Her wages will help pay for gas. A wage is payment in exchange for work. Before looking at job openings online, Julia grabs a notebook. She writes down a few important points.

Many people turn to the internet when looking for jobs.

They are her interests, schedule, and experience. She will use these points to find a job that is right for her.

Julia lists some interests. She likes photography, teaching, and softball. Next, she writes when she is able to work. She can work after school and on weekends.

This means she can work part time.

Part-time work is great for students. It often has flexible schedules. Workers are paid hourly. She can balance her time without getting stressed. If she wants more money, she can work more hours. Finally, Julia thinks about her experience. She has helped coach youth softball teams. She has taken photos for the school yearbook. She writes these items on her list.

Julia is ready to search for jobs. She sits down with her laptop. She goes online and finds a job website. It has a list of open positions. She looks at the list. She notices that teaching jobs require more education than she has. They require college degrees and teaching **licenses**. She is not **qualified** for teaching jobs now. But she could be in the future. She crosses *teaching* off her list. She keeps scrolling. She doesn't see any softball positions open.

Finally, she finds a photography job. It is at her local newspaper. She looks at the description. It requires photography experience. Julia smiles. She has experience with last year's yearbook. Some of those photos would be great examples of her work. It also asks for a cover letter

A résumé is an important part of applying for jobs.

and résumé. A cover letter describes why someone is a good fit for a certain job. A résumé lists the skills and experience that make someone qualified for a job. Julia knows it will take time to finish the cover letter and résumé. But she is excited to apply for this job.

CHAPTER ONE

WHERE CAN I FIND JOB OPENINGS?

People learn about the kinds of jobs they might like in school. They study different subjects. They see what classes interest them. They talk with teachers about job options. All of these experiences help young people decide what career path is right for them. Sometimes students

Many people discover their interests in school. This helps them choose a career.

change paths. They might start studying

one topic. Then they change their mind

after taking a few classes. Switching career

paths is common. People make new goals.

They figure out what type of work they want

to do.

Students often work part time or seasonally to gain work experience.

Different types of jobs give different kinds of flexibility and experience. Full-time work is usually forty hours a week or more. Part-time work is usually less than forty. Seasonal work is only for a certain period of time. Summer vacation and the holiday season are common times for seasonal work. Internships and apprenticeships give people hands-on work experience before they are fully hired. An internship is a temporary job at a company. It can be paid or unpaid. People can see what the work is really like. Internships often help people

WHAT IS AN APPRENTICESHIP?

An apprenticeship is on-the-job training. It is a common first step in **trade jobs** such as carpentry or construction. People do skilled work. They get paid more as their skills get better. Eventually, they graduate from the apprenticeship program. They get a document showing proof of their skills. Then they are often hired as a regular employee.

choose a career path. Michael Carter is a school counselor in Virginia. He says, "I think there's no substitute for any type of work experience. . . . Without experience, it's hard for students to appreciate what type of career they'd like to have."[1]

LOOKING ONLINE

Most job openings are posted online. Anyone using a computer can see them. However, online access makes the job market competitive. Many people can see the postings. Lots of people try to get one job. In a world of online job postings, job search expert Alison Doyle says,

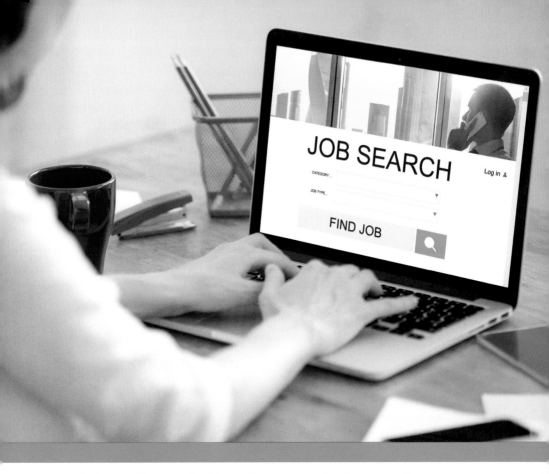

Job posting websites allow people to search for many jobs at once. Jobs can be sorted by location, type of work, and more.

"Job searching is a numbers game. Apply for as many jobs as possible."[2]

There are many job posting websites. These websites show jobs from many companies. They benefit people in several ways. People can browse different openings. They can narrow their job search easily. They can **filter** jobs by their location, salary, and more. People can create a profile. They post their résumé to the site. They show off their skills and experience.

WHAT'S A LINKEDIN PROFILE?

LinkedIn is a social networking site. It can be used for all parts of the job search. Companies post job openings. People can send their résumé to employers. A strong profile has multiple parts. It has contact information. It lists skills. It has a summary of work experiences. People use keywords to describe their work. Keywords stand out to **recruiters**. Recruiters use LinkedIn to find new employees.

Some employers search these websites to find new employees. They can reach out to people with strong profiles.

Another place to look for jobs online is company websites. These websites are great for people who know what company they want to work for. Many company websites have a Careers page. This page shows job openings in the company. People can follow the listed instructions in order to apply for these jobs. People can search for jobs by location, too. They can check local newspaper websites. These websites show jobs in a certain city or town.

People can go to some businesses in person to apply for a job.

FINDING JOBS IN PERSON

While online listings can be quick and easy,

they can also be frustrating. Some people

never get a response after sending an

application. People might look for jobs in

person instead. Companies can advertise

openings with a sign outside. Some have computers to apply on the spot. This is more common for retail or fast food companies. It is usually better to apply online for private businesses.

Networking is another way to look for jobs in person. Networking is exchanging information about the working world. It can happen in everyday conversations. Neighbors talk with each other about work and company news. It can also happen at formal events. A college may put on a dinner for students to meet **alumni**. The event helps students meet new people, which could help them get a job. Many people find out about job openings by talking with others. For this reason, networking can happen in many ways.

To network, people connect with other workers. They talk about work experiences or interests. They ask questions. They learn about what work is like at different companies. Sometimes people share news about job openings. Doyle suggests, "Advertise the fact that you're looking for a job. You never know who might be looking for their next employee. Tell everyone you know that you are looking for a job."[3]

Making connections through networking can help people find jobs.

People can easily network with friends

and family members. They can also talk

with **acquaintances** or strangers who

share things in common. For example, they

might talk to others who graduated from

the same school. Their alumni networks

can connect them. Many college students network to learn about job openings.

SHOULD I GO TO A JOB FAIR?

A job fair is an event to help employers and people meet. Companies send a few employees to the fair. They answer questions about the company. Job seekers have conversations with the employees. Job fairs can lead to an interview or getting hired.

Job fairs have many advantages. They are a chance to network. Job seekers learn more about certain companies. However, job fairs can be stressful. Many people go.

Job fairs give people the opportunity to meet many employers at once.

They wait in long lines. People have to take time off to travel and attend the fair.

People can find a job online. They can network in person. They can ask neighbors or teachers if they know of any job openings. They can go to a job fair. There are many ways to find a job.

CHAPTER TWO

WHAT DO I NEED TO APPLY FOR A JOB?

To apply for a job, you must fill out a job application. The job application has basic information such as a person's name and address. People often need to include a résumé and cover letter. These documents show work experience, education, and skills. People need different

The first step in applying for a job is filling out an application.

levels of education for certain jobs. The

amount of schooling they need depends on

the type of job they want and how much

money they want to earn.

WHAT IS IN A RÉSUMÉ?

A résumé is key to applying for jobs. It

highlights your work experience and skills.

A good résumé is essential to apply for jobs.

It gives employers a big picture of your history at a glance. The purpose of a résumé is to show that you're qualified for the job.

A good résumé is organized into sections. Your name and contact information go at the top of the page. Some people include an objective. The objective explains their goals. They write what job

they hope to get and why. It's only a few

sentences long. An objective is optional.

Education and work experience are next.

They tend to be the largest sections. Many

students put the education section first.

They write what school they go to. They list

their graduation date and GPA. They include awards such as Honor Roll. They also add school clubs or teams they are part of. These activities can impress employers. They show that a person can manage their time. They also show the person's interests.

People who have graduated usually put the work experience section first. They list past and current jobs. They write which companies they worked for. They give short descriptions of what they did at each job. Most people use bullet point lists for tasks. However, your first résumé may look different. You may not have had

Clubs and sports teams can provide important skills to list on a résumé.

any formal jobs. Doyle says, "When writing your first résumé with no work experience, it's appropriate to include casual jobs like babysitting, pet sitting, lawn mowing, and shoveling snow. All experience counts."[4] The key to writing a strong résumé with limited work experience is highlighting skills.

Volunteer work can look good on a résumé.

For example, babysitting shows responsibility. Being captain of a team shows leadership. Stacking shelves shows organization. Use your experiences to show skills that make you a great worker.

The rest of the résumé has volunteer and skill sections. Volunteer work is optional. It can be good work experience. It can also show employers that you care about helping others. The skill section shows hard and soft skills. Hard skills can be measured. Examples of hard skills are speaking a language, driving a car, or knowing how to use a computer. Soft skills are related to

WHY SHOULD I VOLUNTEER?

Volunteering can boost your résumé. Many employers look for people with volunteer experience. Experts found that employers are more likely to hire someone who has volunteer experience than someone who does not. Volunteering helps people in need. It also helps you learn new skills and meet new people. Volunteering can even improve your health. Studies show it helps reduce stress and anxiety. People see how their actions make a difference in the world.

how you work and act. Examples of soft skills include attentive listening, solving problems, or working well with others.

HOW DO I WRITE A COVER LETTER?

A cover letter spells out why you are the best fit for a certain job. It uses paragraphs and a story to show your work experience. It goes beyond the information in your résumé. It fills in the gaps. It gives details about important skills and relates them to the job.

You should write a unique cover letter for each job application. Don't send the same letter to several positions. Cover letters are

Parts of a Cover Letter

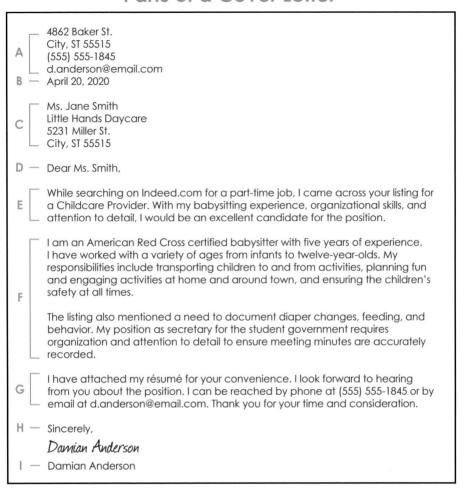

A
4862 Baker St.
City, ST 55515
(555) 555-1845
d.anderson@email.com

B — April 20, 2020

C
Ms. Jane Smith
Little Hands Daycare
5231 Miller St.
City, ST 55515

D — Dear Ms. Smith,

E While searching on Indeed.com for a part-time job, I came across your listing for a Childcare Provider. With my babysitting experience, organizational skills, and attention to detail, I would be an excellent candidate for the position.

F I am an American Red Cross certified babysitter with five years of experience. I have worked with a variety of ages from infants to twelve-year-olds. My responsibilities include transporting children to and from activities, planning fun and engaging activities at home and around town, and ensuring the children's safety at all times.

The listing also mentioned a need to document diaper changes, feeding, and behavior. My position as secretary for the student government requires organization and attention to detail to ensure meeting minutes are accurately recorded.

G I have attached my résumé for your convenience. I look forward to hearing from you about the position. I can be reached by phone at (555) 555-1845 or by email at d.anderson@email.com. Thank you for your time and consideration.

H — Sincerely,

Damian Anderson

I — Damian Anderson

A. Your return address. Be sure to include your contact information.

B. Date line. This should be the date you type the letter.

C. Inside address. This is the name, title, and address of the person you're writing.

D. Greeting line. Try to find the name of the person in charge of hiring for the position. If this information isn't available, use a general title such as "Hiring Manager."

E. Introduction. In this section, you should explain what job you're applying for, where you saw the job listing, and why you'd be a good fit. You'll go into detail in the next paragraph.

F. Body paragraphs. This is the section where you explain how your experience makes you a good candidate for the job. Look at the job listing for what kinds of skills the employer requires. Use this section to explain how your experience is relevant.

G. Closing paragraph. In this section, thank the person reading the letter for her time. You should also give your contact information.

H. Closing. A closing such as "Sincerely," is generally appropriate. Leave space before your identification.

I. Identification. Type your name here. Sign the paper by hand in the space you've left above.

This sample cover letter is from a high school student applying for a job at a daycare.

meant to be specific. Change details in your writing to relate to each position.

EXTRA MATERIALS

Many jobs only require a résumé and cover letter. But people can give more. They can apply with portfolios or references.

WHAT LEVEL OF EDUCATION DO I NEED?

A high school diploma opens up many job opportunities. It is also required by most employers. Teachers can give references. A college degree opens up more options. College degrees are required for some jobs. Some jobs require multiple degrees. People with specialized jobs such as doctors tend to have higher salaries. In the end, people must decide if college is right for them. They should consider costs, their interests, and their career goals.

A portfolio is a collection of work samples. It is a tool people often use to apply for creative jobs. Many people make online portfolios. They create a personal website. They post examples of original work. They put up photos, song lyrics, website designs, and more. People can put a link to their portfolio on their application. Employers can easily see their work.

A reference is someone who speaks positively about your skills. It's someone you have worked with. For example, imagine Nick is hiring a new assistant. He reads Tessa's résumé and cover letter. She helped

Teachers and bosses are examples of people who can provide references.

coach a soccer team. He wants to know

more about that job. Tessa listed references

on the bottom of her résumé. May was the

head coach of the team. He calls her. May

tells him Tessa was organized. She was

always on time. She even emailed parents

about schedules. Those skills are important

for an assistant. Nick decides to hire Tessa.

Talking to May convinced him Tessa is a

good worker. If you include references

on your résumé, be sure to tell the person

from whom you're asking for a reference.

You don't want them to be surprised by a

phone call.

References can also write a letter for

you. Some applications require reference

letters. Reference letters tell why you

would be a good fit for a job. They back up

your résumé.

CHAPTER THREE

HOW DO I APPLY FOR A JOB?

The ways to apply for jobs have changed over time. People used to only apply in person. They knocked on doors. They spoke directly to employers. Companies would post job openings in newspapers. People might call or visit places with openings. It was harder to apply for jobs in a different city than it is today.

Reading ads in the newspaper or making phone calls used to be the most common way to find jobs. Now, most people use the internet.

Computers changed how people apply for jobs. Today, it is less common to give applications in person. Applying online is faster and easier. People don't have to travel. They can send in their application at any time. Many companies prefer to get applications online. They can easily view

lots of applications. They can reply quickly

by email.

   While viewing online applications, many

employers check people's social media.

One employer said, "It tells so much more

than a résumé ever could."[5] Employers see

WATCH YOUR SOCIAL MEDIA!

Employers often check people's social media. They look for inappropriate content. They don't want to hire people with negative posts. You should take down old posts with inappropriate words or images. Always think before you post.

   Social media can also boost your application. You can express your creativity. You can connect with companies online. You can share about topics you're interested in.

people's pictures and posts. They learn

about people's interests and personality.

They see if someone has the same values

as the company. Expert Michelle Armer

says, "Before applying to jobs, students

should clean up their social media

accounts."[6] A study found that 70 percent of

employers use social media for research. Of

those employers, 57 percent found content

that stopped them from hiring someone.

FILLING OUT AN APPLICATION

Once you find a job you're interested

in, it's time to apply. When filling out an

application, it's important to follow all the

It's important to accurately and completely fill out applications.

directions. Be sure to include any forms

the company asks for. They often want a

résumé and cover letter.

Sometimes the application repeats

information on the résumé. It may ask

for contact information. It may ask for

dates and names of past jobs. Be sure to fill out all parts of the required forms. Leaving blank sections shows a lack of effort. Employers may think you are not serious about applying. They may not read incomplete applications.

TIPS FOR APPLYING

Use positive responses. Don't make up answers. For example, an application might ask about a certain computer program. Don't lie about working with the program. Be truthful about your skills. Then add a positive explanation. Mention your excitement to learn the program.

Give an example of how you are a quick learner. Employers value honesty. They may not expect you to know the program beforehand. They know they can train you to learn new skills.

Many people hurry to finish their application. They don't check the spelling and grammar. But small mistakes can add up. You should reread your application before sending it. Make sure your answers are clear.

Some people add colored font to their résumé. Color makes their application stand out. It also shows creativity. But

Checking for spelling errors is important for résumés and cover letters.

using too much color can be distracting.

Make sure the font is clear. People should

be able to read it easily. You could ask a

family member or friend to look at your

application. Get their opinion on the design.

When in doubt, use black and white. Clean

Sometimes companies take a while to respond to an application. Waiting can feel frustrating.

and simple designs are safe. Employers

will stay focused on the writing instead of

the design.

WHEN WILL I HEAR BACK?

Once the application is sent in, it's time to wait. Most people hear back in a couple of weeks. Employers take time to think about which applications are best. Sometimes multiple people review each application. Some companies respond quickly. Others take more time. Large companies tend to take longer. They have to look through many applications.

If you do not hear back soon, you may want to contact the company to follow up. You have to decide when is the right time to reach out. Waiting too long gives other people a chance to contact the company first. But asking about your application too soon can annoy employers. The right time to reach out is different for each situation. Some jobs have an application deadline. This date lets you know when the company will start looking at applications. Be sure to wait until after the deadline to ask about your application. Other jobs have no deadline. The company could look at applications any time. Some experts say waiting one week is long enough. Other people reach out after two weeks. Since most people hear back in a couple

People can follow up on their job application by phone or by email.

of weeks, these times are appropriate.

Sometimes a job posting will say, "No

phone calls, please." In this case, do not

follow up. If you do, it shows you can't

follow directions.

Many people decide to email instead of

call. Employers can look at emails any time.

They can respond when they are ready.

An email leaves information in writing.

Employers will see your name again. They

can easily contact you. Experts recommend

sending your résumé and cover letter again.

WRITING A FOLLOW-UP EMAIL

When sending a follow-up email, experts recommend a short message. The message starts with your name. It says what job you are applying for. Then one or two sentences talk about your main skill. They remind the employer why they should hire you. The message ends with a thank you. It could say, "For your reference, I'm attaching my cover letter and résumé. I have also applied online. I sincerely appreciate your time and look forward to hearing from you."

"Q&A: How Long Should You Wait to Hear Back About a Job?" Indeed Career Guide, n.d., http://indeed.com.

Attaching these documents makes it easy for employers. They might read your email and want to know more about you. If your résumé is handy, they are more likely to read it.

The employer will reach out if they are interested. They may email or call. Sometimes employers never respond if they are not interested. Not hearing back can be frustrating. People have to stay positive. They can look for other jobs at any time. They don't have to wait to hear back to apply somewhere else.

CHAPTER FOUR

HOW DOES A JOB INTERVIEW WORK?

An interview is a meeting. An employer talks with someone who wants a job. Employers ask questions. Some are about the person's work experience. Others are about his or her strengths and weaknesses. Sometimes employers ask what the person likes to do

A job interview is a chance to meet in person with a potential employer.

for fun. Interviews help people get to know one another. They show whether the person is a good fit for the company. Job search site Workopolis says being a good fit "is what it sounds like. Do you, as a person, align with the company's values? Does it seem like you would gel with the current company culture?"[7]

Some companies have an interview process. The process could include multiple meetings. Some first interviews are done on the phone or with video chat. They help the company decide if the person should come to the office. In-person interviews are more serious. They often happen later in the process. Some interview processes include skill tests. For example, writers may have to complete a writing test. Skills tests show the company a specific example of your work.

In the end, the process leads to a company hiring someone.

HOW SHOULD I PREPARE FOR MY INTERVIEW?

One way to prepare is researching the company. Look at all parts of its website. Take notes. Write down any questions you have. Employers often let people ask

WHAT DO I WEAR TO AN INTERVIEW?

Employers meet you for the first time at an interview. You want to make a good impression. Be sure to groom your hair. Looking neat and clean shows that you care. You should wear dress clothes. Look at the company's website to see what type of clothes are appropriate. Dressing too formally is better than dressing too casually.

It's important to do research on a company before going to an interview.

questions in the interview. Having a few

questions ready shows you are interested in

the company. It also shows you spent time

learning more about the job.

Another way to prepare for an interview is

to practice. People can find lists of common

interview questions online. They can think

about their responses beforehand. Some

people make notes while they practice.

They don't want to forget their answers.

They can list their strengths. They might

write important work experiences they have.

Many colleges have career centers.

They help students find and apply for jobs.

They let people do mock interviews. A

mock interview is practice. You schedule

a meeting with someone from the center.

You arrive wearing professional clothes.

The person asks you questions like an

employer would. You answer as if it were a

real interview. Afterward, you and the center expert talk about what went well. He or she gives you tips for the future. Many people feel more confident after doing mock interviews. Doyle says, "Practice interviews familiarize users with the interview process and allow users to practice answering common interview questions with confidence."[8]

Finally, make sure you know the location, time, and date of the interview. Calling to double-check the time is better than getting it wrong. Missing an interview may lead to not getting the job. Some people print an

Many colleges have career centers. These centers provide resources and can help with résumés, cover letters, and practice interviews.

extra copy of their résumé. They bring it

with them to the interview. Instead of folding

it in their pocket, they may keep it in a

folder. The paper stays flat and neat. They

might also bring samples of their work.

Being on time, dressing professionally, and being polite can help make an interview successful.

MY INTERVIEW IS TODAY! WHAT SHOULD I DO?

Experts recommend arriving ten to fifteen minutes early. Being early shows responsibility. It also gives people a chance to focus. Being late can make people stressed. It also isn't professional. A person's behavior can affect the interview. Being calm and friendly helps. People shake hands. They smile at one another. Rude behavior hurts people's chances of getting hired. Staring down at a phone can be rude. Chewing gum can be distracting.

People also get ready early for phone and video interviews. They find a quiet space. They get out any notes they made. They have a pen and paper in case they need to schedule a future interview. During the interview, they listen carefully to questions before answering. They take their time talking. They try not to say *ah* or *um*. They don't talk too fast. In video interviews, people make sure to look at the camera when speaking.

Each job interview is different. Some companies start with phone or video interviews. They might include multiple meetings or skills tests. Other companies just do one in-person interview. For these reasons, you should ask questions if the interview process isn't clear. Employers can tell you what to expect. Then, it's up to you to prepare and do your best.

SENDING A THANK YOU NOTE

After an interview, people follow up. They may reach out a few days later. They call, email, or send a thank you note in the mail. People remind the employer of one or two skills. Most of all, they thank the company for taking time to interview them. Thank you notes show extra care. Employers often get more emails than personal notes. Thank you notes can help a person stand out.

CHAPTER FIVE

I GOT A JOB OFFER! NOW WHAT?

A person from the company will reach out to formally offer a job. In a phone call, you should first thank the person for the offer. Next, listen for details. You may have to go to the office to sign paperwork. Someone may send you an email with more information. Before hanging

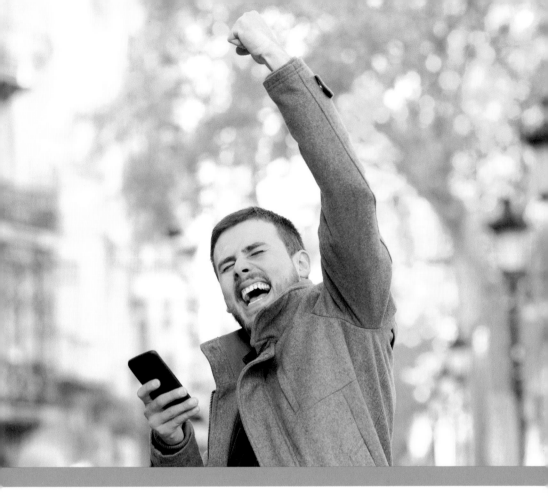

Getting a job offer can be an exciting moment.

up, ask any questions you have. In an email

offer, people can respond right away so the

company knows they received the offer. But

they don't have to accept it. They can take

a few days to think about it.

WHAT'S IN A JOB OFFER?

A job offer describes the tasks the person will do. It also lists the hours the company expects the person to work. Then it shows what the person will be paid. This can be an hourly wage or a salary. A wage is money paid per hour. Paychecks change depending on how much someone works. Hourly work can be unreliable. People make less money if there is less work to do. On the other hand, people can work more if they want to make extra money.

A salary is the total amount of money someone will be paid in a year. Salaried employees could work thirty-five hours one week. They could work forty-five hours another. But their paychecks would be the same. Some people feel secure getting regular paychecks. Other people worry they

NEGOTIATING A JOB OFFER

When people aren't satisfied with a job offer, they can negotiate. Negotiating is discussing other options. It could include getting paid more. It could mean getting more vacation days. A counteroffer is a suggestion of what you think is fair. People do research. They can look up what other people get for doing similar work. Research helps people make an appropriate counteroffer. People often call a meeting to negotiate in person.

Health insurance is one of many benefits often offered by companies to full-time employees.

will work too much. Companies don't have to pay them more for working extra.

Benefits are another way companies pay employees. Full-time jobs often have benefits. Benefits include paid time off for illness or vacation. They may also include retirement and **insurance** plans. A retirement plan saves money for when you stop working. Benefits can make a big difference for families. Vacation time lets parents spend time with their kids. Insurance plans help pay for medical bills.

THINKING ABOUT AN OFFER

Accepting a job is an important decision. People need to know what they are agreeing to. They can ask detailed questions. They can ask about their schedule. People can also ask to meet their boss or other employees. Take your time thinking about the offer. All parts of the job matter. Remember to think about your larger career goals, too.

In the end, people decide to accept or decline the offer. They may accept knowing it is a step toward their dream job. They may decline because the work isn't worth the payment. Either way, it is important to be polite.

HOW DO I TURN DOWN A JOB OFFER?

Many people turn down offers on the phone or in an email. They choose the way they are most comfortable with. First, they thank the company. They name specific people they communicated with. They acknowledge the time people spent considering them. Next, they give a clear but quick reason for declining. For example, they might say, "It's not quite the right fit for my career goals at this time." Finally, they wish the employer well in the future.

Finding a job can be a long process. But accepting an offer makes it worth the effort.

Finding a job isn't easy. It takes multiple steps. Ideally, the search ends with a job offer. When people accept a job offer, they see how their search was worth the hard work and effort.

WORKSHEET

BUILD YOUR OWN RÉSUMÉ

Practice making your own résumé. Your résumé should include:

- Your name and contact information

- Education section

- Experience section

You can also include:

- Objective or summary statement

- Awards/accomplishments section

- Volunteer section

- Skills—hard and soft

See the example provided for an idea of how to format your résumé.

Your Name

1243 Address St. City, ST 55515 | (555) 555-1375 | name@email.com | Website or LinkedIn profile

This section is where you can put your objective or summary statement. It should be two to three sentences.

Education

General Diploma | City High School; City, ST   Expected May 2022
- GPA: 3.5
- Clubs: Debate Team (president), National Honor Society, Marching Band (section leader)
- Honors: Honor roll, school service award (2020)

Experience

Grocery Store | City, ST   June 2020–Present
Cashier
- Worked to efficiently check out customers' groceries, answer questions, and accurately count change.
- Unloaded inventory trucks and followed corporate directives to stock merchandise in a visually appealing way.

Smith Household | City, ST   Sept. 2019–Present
Babysitter
- Supervised children ages five through twelve. Duties included playing games, cooking meals, and transporting them to activities.
- Completed CPR certification to ensure maximum safety training.

Skills

- Time management
- Organization
- Attention to detail
- Money management
- Customer service
- Leadership
- Public speaking
- Teamwork
- Communication

Volunteer Work
- Tutoring children at the library
- Serving once a month at the local soup kitchen

GLOSSARY

acquaintances

people someone knows but isn't very close to

alumni

people who have graduated from a certain college

benefits

another way a company pays its employees, such as time off and health insurance

filter

to remove something unwanted or unrelated

insurance

a type of business agreement people can buy so that the company will pay for certain unexpected damages or bills

licenses

documents people get to prove skills for their job

qualified

when someone has finished the education or experience required for a job

recruiters

people who search for new people to hire

trade jobs

skilled labor such as plumbing or carpentry

SOURCE NOTES

CHAPTER ONE: WHERE CAN I FIND JOB OPENINGS?

1. Quoted in Elka Torpey, "Career Planning for High Schoolers," *Bureau of Labor Statistics*, January 2015. http://bls.gov.

2. Alison Doyle, "Job Search Tips for High School Students," *The Balance Careers*, May 15, 2019. http://thebalancecareers.com.

3. Doyle, "Job Search Tips for High School Students."

CHAPTER TWO: WHAT DO I NEED TO APPLY FOR A JOB?

4. Alison Doyle, "First Resume Example with No Work Experience," *The Balance Careers*, February 13, 2019. http://thebalancecareers.com.

CHAPTER THREE: HOW DO I APPLY FOR A JOB?

5. Quoted in Jill Cornfield, "Simple Ways to Craft a Perfect Social Profile for Job Hunting," *CNBC*, June 14, 2019. http://cnbc.com.

6. Quoted in Abigail Hess, "7 Steps College Students Can Take Now to Set Themselves Up for a High-Paying Career after Graduation," *CNBC*, June 27, 2019. http://cnbc.com.

CHAPTER FOUR: HOW DOES A JOB INTERVIEW WORK?

7. "Not Your Dad's Job Market: How to Job Search in the 21st Century," *Workopolis*, October 20, 2016. http://careers.workopolis.com.

8. Alison Doyle, "An Overview of Mock Interviews," *The Balance Careers*, November 15, 2018. http://thebalancecareers.com.

FOR FURTHER RESEARCH

BOOKS

Stephen Currie, *Teen Guide to Jobs and Taxes*. San Diego, CA: ReferencePoint Press, 2017.

Kara McGuire, *All About the Green: The Teens' Guide to Finding Work and Making Money*. North Mankato, MN: Capstone, 2015.

Sarah Pawlewski, *Careers: The Graphic Guide to Finding the Perfect Job for You*. New York: DK Publishing, 2015.

INTERNET SOURCES

Alison Doyle, "Cover Letter Layout Example and Formatting Tips," *The Balance Careers*, June 18, 2019. www.thebalancecareers.com.

Alison Doyle, "Job Interview Tips for High School Students," *The Balance Careers*, February 27, 2019. www.thebalancecareers.com.

"High School Resume Tips and Example," *Indeed.com*, n.d. www.indeed.com/career-advice.

Thad Peterson, "100 Top Job Interview Questions—Be Prepared for the Interview," *Monster.com*, n.d. www.monster.com/career-advice.

WEBSITES

GetMyFuture
www.careeronestop.org/GetMyFuture

The US Department of Labor runs this website. It has a variety of resources, including information about job listings, writing a résumé, and going to college.

Indeed
www.indeed.com

Indeed allows users to browse hundreds of jobs. Users can filter jobs based on location, salary, and more.

My Next Move
www.mynextmove.org

My Next Move helps users explore jobs related to their interests. The site provides information such as what level of education is needed for a particular career, salary information, and more.

INDEX

applications, 18, 24, 32, 35, 37,
  39–40, 41–48
apprenticeships, 13

benefits, 67, 68–69

clothes, 55, 57
cover letters, 8–9, 24, 32–33, 34,
  35–36, 42, 50–51

deadlines, 48
design, 44–46
Doyle, Alison, 14–15, 20, 29, 58

education, 7–8, 10–11, 24–25,
  27–28, 34
emails, 39–40, 49–51, 63,
  64–65, 70

following up, 47–49, 50, 63
full-time work, 12, 68

hard skills, 31

insurance, 68–69
internships, 13–14
interviews, 22, 52–54, 55–59,
  61–63

job fairs, 22–23
job offers, 64–65, 66–68, 69–71

licenses, 8
LinkedIn, 16

mock interviews, 57–58

networking, 16, 19–23

part-time work, 7, 12
paychecks, 66–67
portfolios, 34–35
preparation, 55–59

qualifications, 8–9, 26

references, 34–37
résumés, 8–9, 16, 24–32, 34–37,
  40, 42, 44, 50–51, 58–59

salary, 16, 66–67
seasonal work, 12–13
social media, 40–41
soft skills, 31–32

trade jobs, 13

volunteering, 30–31

wages, 5, 66
work experience, 13–14, 16, 20, 24,
  25, 27–30, 32, 52, 57

IMAGE CREDITS

ABOUT THE AUTHOR

Emma Huddleston lives in Minnesota with her husband. She enjoys writing children's books, swing dancing, and running.